Oneiroscope

ONEIROSCOPE

STEPHEN SUNDERLAND

KU PRESS

First published in 2023 by Kingston University Press

A catalogue of this book is available from the British Library.

ISBN 978 1 909362 70 3

Typeset in IM FELL DW Pica

Photographs © Stephen Sunderland

Editorial and Design by Kingston University MA Publishing Students:
Tara Hiralal
Maja Kristiansen
Tal Rejwan
Farah Nadia Zulkiflee

KINGSTON UNIVERSITY PRESS
Kingston University
Penrhyn Road
Kingston-upon-Thames
KT1 2EE

Twitter @stephensunderla
Mastodon @Corsairsanglot@mastodon.social

Preface

The early Surrealists enjoyed nothing more than going into film screenings at random moments, staying for an unspecified length of time or until boredom kicked in, before leaving with half-remembered fragments of the films; from which they would assemble a new version, free of logic and purpose.

Oneiroscope speaks to that time at the birth of Surrealism, in the early days of cinema, a time of great uncertainty much like our own. The oneiroscope itself is what Paul Nougé might have described as an 'objet bouleversant' – something which, if believed in and acceded to, has the capacity to change the meaning of things as they are.

The poems were written gradually during lockdown and beyond, a period in which time seemed to bend and stretch, and fragments of film and reading matter took up weird and distorted significance. It was also the time I had allotted to write a surrealist film-novel, *The Cinema Beneath the Lake*, about a cinema capable of transmitting the unconscious of its occupants. My creative life and real life felt like they were fused during this time of confusion, isolation and fear.

A film that took up odd significance was *Max, Mon Amour*; its story capable of inducing a fever dream at the best of times. But here, during this unprecedented period of catastrophe, I was drawn to its deadpan recounting of a remarkable, surreal encounter between human and chimpanzee. I was particularly drawn to the actor of Max, who played the chimpanzee uncannily well, my eyes drawn to her eyes behind the make-up and prosthetics where she was busy thinking and reacting.

This came to be something of an obsession for me. I was fascinated by the idea of being in a dream-film, of transformations and inbetween-ness, of how it might be to look out through the eye-holes of a mask. Max became a symbol of what was going on in the world at this time and I found his presence haunting the frame of my thinking, merging oddly with it, as these poems reveal.

Oneiroscope (n.)

Resembling the kinétoscope, (the early 20th
century crank-handled machine into which
the viewer would squint to watch a short
sequence of moving images) the oneiroscope
offered the same experience using radically
different source material: dreams.

Let the film begin

           in the dark artery

                      underground

A hundred globes
of liquid

              burst

                    into forward motion

flow out
as cars

                          Surge

            into
            light

We're in a schoolroom
with the kids

from *Zéro de Conduite*

Blizzard of goose feathers

This could be happening as we:

CROSS into

digital

aphasia

athambia

apathia:

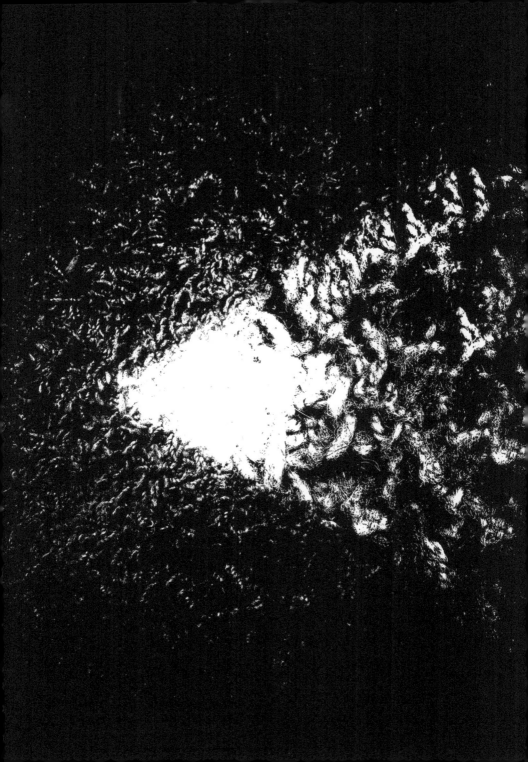

Les Détraquées

Over a panoply of smashed landscapes & the whimper of curs:

Tenth arrondissement
                    we watch amongst clutter
                                        of corks, breadcrumbs

                slack-jawed observers
of our picnic half blocking
                                        the stage for moments

                aiding the détournement

The trail of the octopus
                                        lead me a merry dance –
                now this

A balloon falls
                                        What happens when it
                                                    lands?
Anything. It's true.

                                        In the ghost castle, bleached
                                                    walls

                                        flashes of itinerant-me

CROSS TO:

IRIS OUT:

Un tableau vivant –

At one time, I live in Italy
in a single-storey building,
assistant to a popular singer
who keeps me, her familiar,
as some sort of slave, uses me
to indulge her passions, wearing
a velour all-in-one jumpsuit.

We live in a giant four-poster
somehow on its roof, another
stage, close to the ceiling.
I'm rarely out of bed, always
seemingly undressed. When I try
to get dressed, either I have no
clothes or can never find them ➤

We are preparing for the launch
of her new book. Her fans are coming:
I'm to usher them to their seats,
offer free wine, shepherd them
towards the book stall. It's baking hot,
I'm sweating as I mind the guests, who
admire me, regardless – I'm her assistant!

At last, I slip away from the crowd.
I've been naked for too long and
I find a giant football shirt,
the colours of Italy's national team.
It fits me like a coal sack. I run
across the hot stones of the roadway, miles
to go to reach my children.

Where are they?

HIKE SPOOL TO:

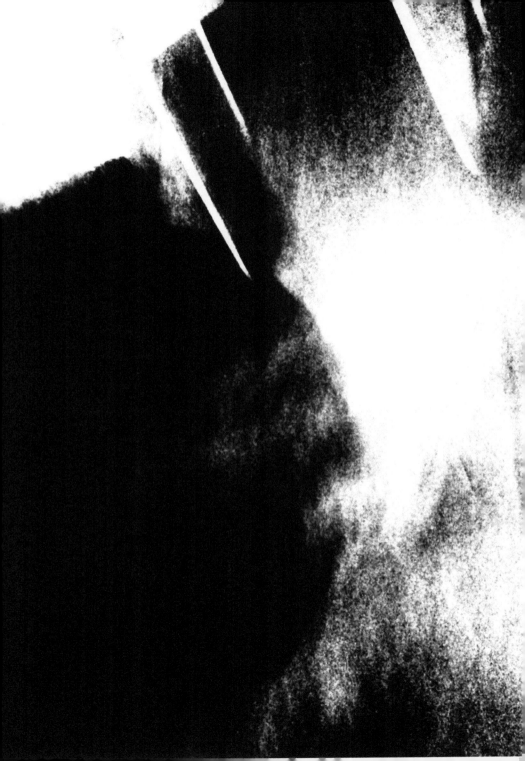

Tenth arrondissement

hushed auditorium

The picnic is finished

An empty wine-bottle
rolls down the aisle

SMASHES

in the orchestra pit

A chimpanzee-man
gambols on stage
settles on a three-
legged stool

begins to speak:

TRACK IN to the EYES:

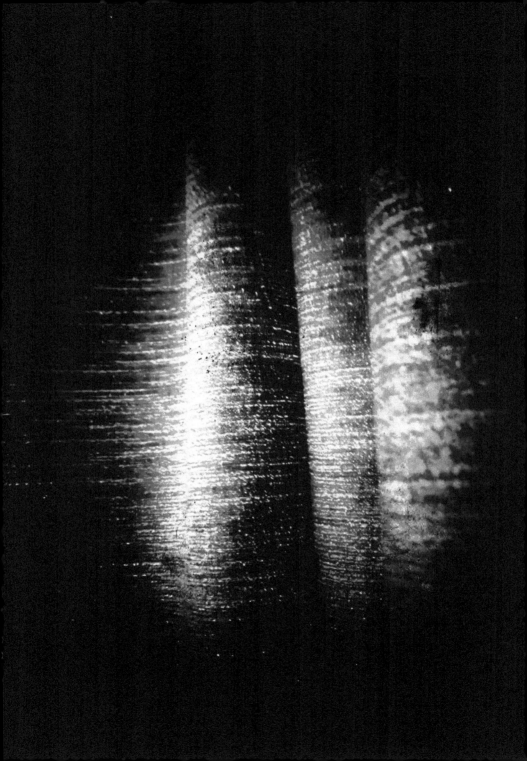

The Song of Max

I tried my best to be an animal; yours.
  Part simian, part reptile, twinned
   with my own clown at birth.

Sometimes I got between myselves
  and into your plan for me.
   Other times I watched from eyeholes.

You: a cruel technicolour angel,
  sleek in impossible fashions,
   scarlet as blood, green as earth.

I never loved you, how could I?
  You put me in a cage at dinner,
   believed those accounts of my antics

This was a story of you and yours
the blond perfect son like Jesus
the liberal husband, reason incarnate

It could never escape its progeny
this Victorian fable dressed up
a touch of Darwin, Sade, Lautréamont

No kin of mine could thrive here.
I eat your food because I must;
I entertain your ménage à trois,

knowing the cops were always running
through the woods with their dogs
to detain our imagined children.

Un ange passe

He skulks away
in silence

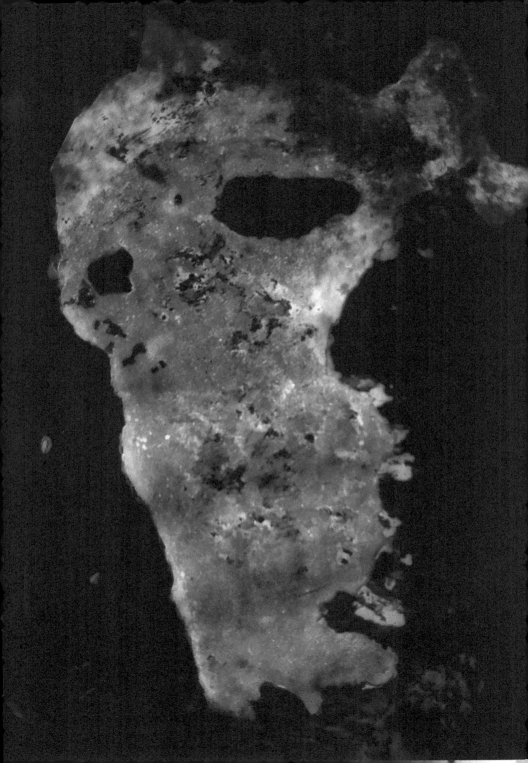

Something unworldly

troubles the lens,

AND:

A creature – part insect,

part bird, part sky –

flitters onstage

Hardly a song

more a careening of air ➤

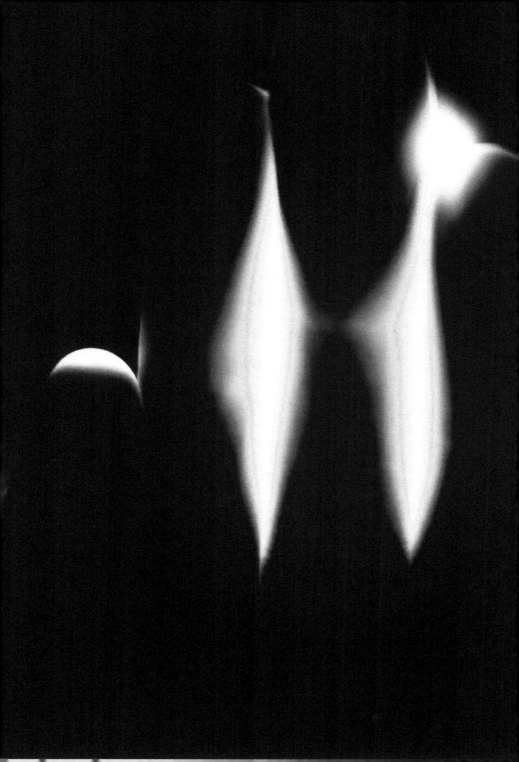

The sky-bird-insect

clings

to the CURTAINS

stage-left, swaying.
TRACK IN on the
DELICATE

BLUE BEAK

as it sings ☞

Storm Harvest

Always with purpose
                    a shoal of light
a cloudburst.

            After —
                    we comb the streets
        blister of jellyfish.

            How spritely —
                        bags of numbers
        rub between our thighs.

            Chirruping crickets
                        we keep warm
        between words.

            New skin
        tender to the touch,
                    old memories of dawn ➥

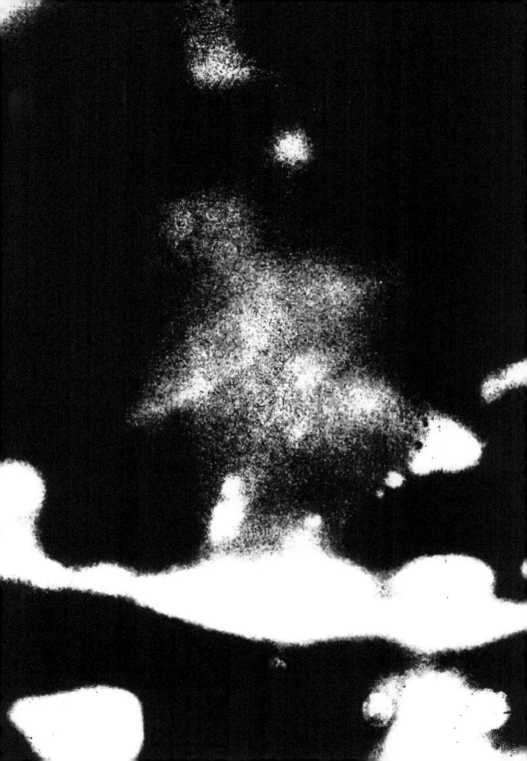

Clouds close,
a medley of fractions.
Sensing threat, we

skip inside.
Friction between vectors
makes its song.

This is how music
will sound
in a thousand years.

QUICK BLACK

FADE UP:

Tenth arrondissement.
Very unsettled.

Queasy.
How long is time?
A Month in the Evening.

I pull a sleeve inside out
to look at the lining and

find a new world there:

An underwater town,
where I enrol on

the Future Leader training programme.

It is a pleasant and eye-opening event. I learned that
a mole
is a reflection in the window
of *objects in another room*.

My son dreams of the kidnap dummy
and a Lego-man with a hot hand on his face.
He's high up, scared of falling.
I have gone away
to get my case.

Are there videos of dreams? he asks.

DISSOLVE TO:

GHOST RIDE through an empty suburban house.
It's mid-winter outside.

The Tall Police

Max measures the boys
to make sure they haven't grown.
Son 1 tells forbidden stories of an independent future to Son 2.

The Tall Police arrive at 3
in the morning to make their arrests.
The boys flee the apocalypse, to their cardboard den in the attic.

Son 1, though older,
won't share the den with a spider.

Son 2 says the spider might help them –
after all, spiders know everything about staying small.

They barricade themselves in.

The Tall Police wait it out, using a

megaphone to check the boys' growth rate ☞

Son 1 goes into hyper sleep,
clevers his brain into
inventing a key card to escape.

Son 2 is a cyber-hacker!

They hack their father's brain,
force him to rob a bank.

He's arrested
and thrown in jail. In the confusion, they

evade
The Tall Police;
bring back supplies.

Now there'll be crimes
of height.
Correction-candy.
Barricaded,
they must survive inside their castle

forever

SMASH-CUT TO:

CLOSE UP

of a painting:
a sky deepens to black;
      below grows blue cosmos
in deep-shallow space –
     meaty red collision with street,
white-yellow of broken egg –

    – arrested in flight
        through a sky entangled
with the undersea markings
        of octopus and coral
living-inanimate fusions
      ever-moving disappearing
re-appearing the triumph
of air

        Prometheus
         a gesture
against canonisation
     a centrifuge, a cosmic oven
alembic dispersal of the body
     seeking its own exit

           DISSOLVE TO:

Tenth arrondissement.
Where did the stage go?

Somehow:
bird's-eye view of a room,
its ceiling removed.

A buzzard's view.

On the blankets, Max sings –

Tryst

Curled together,
we dream
on this flint-torn mattress,
twitchy as jumping beans

in a tapestry rich
with little deaths,
perfect grafts.

You move your arm
to my shoulder and
cloud-shadow chases itself
over crests coming inshore ➤

I recall how
on verdant pavements
                    I walked upright,

        taking in the height and light

of the mottled boulevards
                    in their many disguises;

            back to all fours
only for passing trams
                    and their gogglers, craning.

        You shake me awake,
your eyes a wonder
                    exploding far off.

Where have you been, my love? you ask.

BLACK

FADE UP:

Tenth arrondissement, half-light.

SOUNDS of rustling paper. Sighs.

Max searches through a pile of paper
spread across a space resembling
an attic crossed with a Japanese sitting room.

He's looking for the work of a class
he's meant to be teaching at this exact moment.

He grabs a battered briefcase and exits ➤

The class waits for him in stony silence.
He sits at a corner desk to work.

To his right, a girl studies, intently. When
he looks again, she's been replaced by a

woman smartly dressed in tweed who may,
                              in fact, be a man.

Just as he has accepted this may be the girl
a little older, she tears off her mask,

                pleased her disguise has worked.

Now the lesson is outside in the dark on a
grass slope by an emergency exit.

                        A caretaker comes out,
                a deep-sea diver with a torch,

hails Max to ask what he's doing out here.

He explains, awkwardly, in front of the
class.

CUT TO BLACK

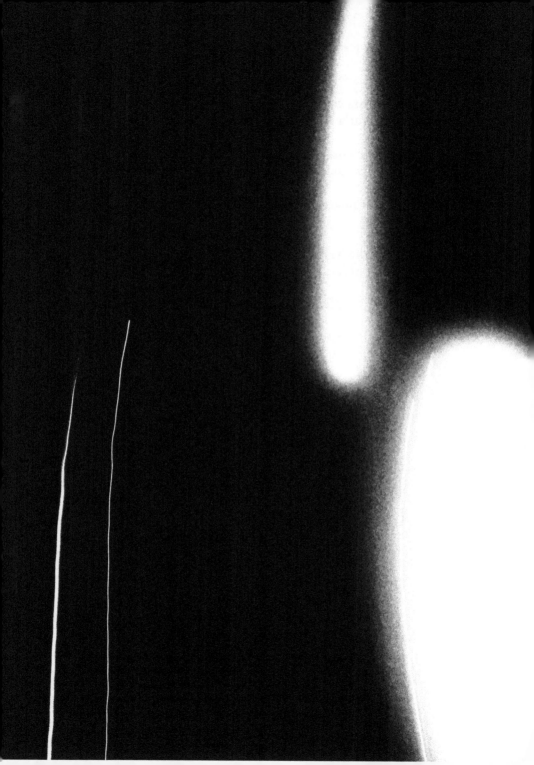

FADE UP:

Somewhere here, a century of tears, THEN:

Whose voice?

The carriage brings him
right to the centre of

                    the night, the room dark,
                    matter finding its home.

He manifests a nursery
of objects and in them

                    his past at all points,
                    singing from the half-light,

never certain if these
atomic frequencies want

                    to make voices, or throw
                    shapes together, hold them ➛

He dreams of the fall
backwards from form,

                              converging with the texture
                              of things; becoming timber,

fat grain of oak
on the arms of his old

                              drinking chair where he tried
                              to disappear on certain days.

SOUND of water rising to fill the space, darkening and –

CUT TO:

DARKNESS: a voice –

I catch a kiss from you, sideways,
without bursting into flames.
All night the ship at sea.

STAY IN BLACK

FADE UP:

A moving tapestry, painted in blood, slowly catches fire through the following TALE:

The magician gave away his tricks.

It was early morning and he walked into the oncoming sun.

Flecks of black burning skin.

The people asked where he was going, charred umbrella.

They watched him go, blinded, sockets asplinter.

Halfway to the burning ball, his skeleton rested.

CROSS TO:

On STAGE: An INFERNO on a marble concourse, shoppers oblivious.

TRACK IN on the FURNACE, shoppers shopping, as *you* sing:

myocarditis tachycardia treble triple tribble trouble rubble ripple roubles
sated fated rated shades in the efterpool genuinely good intentions
tensions infus-ions contorted

axminster dementia fever of souls leaving the weft & warp of moth-holes
as maps in chronos pockets of gum-stuff silken sachets of imposture
thrown on

you would jump at each beam of light, each morsel or parcel, production
of bubbles, fine gradations between safety and diffuse self-interest, shaped
as a life lived now

easy to proceed this way, crossing the river on pebbles...

CUT TO:

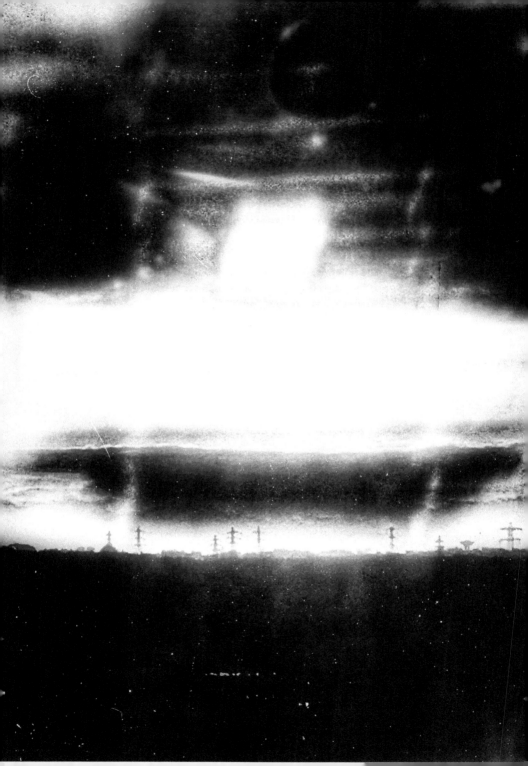

A salty seadog SHOUTS into the drowned lens:

Swab the main deck!

The sea is a curse returning us by way of the indifferent moon.

QUICK BLACK:

FADE UP:

We're in a sterile institution. Max is collecting a sheaf of hand-outs from the photocopier. A blurred figure calls after him, holding up some spare sheets:

Is this yours? Are you Aimé? Aimé Césaire?

[Watch out, Max: beware the moment where you step, not knowing who, why, what, when, how – from your skin, voice afloat, and answer]:

Yes, I'm Aimé Césaire

                                  & I claim my right to négritude, though white-
                                             mannered and book-

ish, glutted with wrong reading so to speak
like a martyr which

                                  I do, with style, in mirrors. You've seen me
                                           looking over at your

grief taking notes com-paring: me, you, white,
black, géo-politique, you

                                losing at winning me winning at losing, sin-
                                       ning. Black as sin. Don't

call me white, I'm grey at best, tidemarked. It's
ok to talk yourself out of

                                one hole but there's no other burrow, fur-lined
                                        or abandoned, no voice
to guide you in.

Max takes the sheaf of copies, runs with them.

SMASH CUT TO:

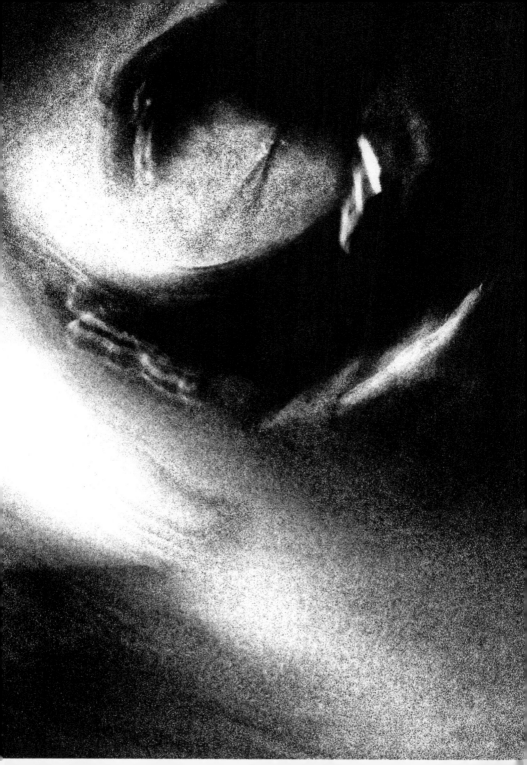

In his basement, Max crouches delivering these words to a cobweb –

TRACK IN on his SPITTLE:

Aimé. *Loved.* I loved
                          he loved she loved we
                                              loved they loved. You
loved, living now,
                                              con-vuls-ive-ly, flexed
                          lens of the machine
that captures you,
                                              in time, patiently,
waiting for day.

I want to break
                          things when I speak
                                              I speak chalk turds
dropped overnight.
                          Not mine! I say,
but stay to check text-
                                              -ure and yes it's mine

so how to stop speak-
                          ing shit? is why I'm
                                              here and there seems
no way out no way out
                          not without brain cuts
not without being left
                                              out like a dog injected
with heroin not with-
                          out a broken jaw so
                                              I cannot speak unwired.

what I would say
what I would say
is this:

The SPITTLE, a whole globe of fury, detaches and FALLS.

QUICK BLACK:

FADE UP:

Pink morning. The storm clouds have gone.

The sky is laced with constellations: bones through skin.

This is some notable planetarium. The STAGE is a smoking ruin.

Over the tattoo of stars, a VOICE:

World of Wonder

The information paradox:
  when you're sucked into
    a black hole your facts
disappear and you return

as a horse, youngish, insouc-
  -iant. You go on in the
    universe differently,
fetlocks tracing a string

theory unfretting its braid,
  to the first symbolic gesture.
    I could sing in Russian,
we could dance, each move

unmaking us, turning you into
  the famous dancing horse of
    the soft hair; our double-helix
tracing its deathless, looping seal.

FADE TO:

Tenth arrondissement.
A plague on all these houses.
Chimpanzee-man has broken cover.

A little while ago he drifted
to the front of the stage
and now: here he is,

staring out past us
to some nether world
out on the streets.

He's removed his MASK.

His human face seems familiar
but I can't make out his features.

He's speaking:

Disavowed

Dressed in white and in love,
                Max thinks he has it all.
Oblivious to the dancer tangled

              and tangling in his wires, he
holds the lead, almost
                 on time, for once.

When he jumps off a bridge or
              into sky, he describes in the air
whatever is attached to him:

      it might be a shape half-intended
              but most likely it will not be
the snapdragon he had in mind.

                             CUT TO:

FADE UP:

Tenth arrondissement.

        Max is at the detonation site

outside the theatre – hoping to bring rubble

    down around his ears as he sits watching from his dust-bubble.

Any infinitesimal adjustment to his proposition

            will cause it to wilt like a cut flower,

back to the mush of loam.

SMASH CUT TO:

Tenth arrondissement.
On stage, Max: asleep, eyes open.
A sound of TICKING,
like a bomb,
over the following VOICE:

Earlier, taking in the evening air on his balcony, he'd missed the baleful alarm
and now everywhere the traipsing feet, the baggage,

taxis to the airport for the final flight to heaven or wherever was a cheap
destination at this late hour.

What he saw of them that day and indeed on all the others at some point
told him they were pretending, almost entirely, with full hope of never
being seen

to be concealed beneath their cosmetics in appreciation of the
pathetic fallacy or whatever other form of wound their lovers
would suppose they chose, to please him.

As long as they knew he had tried, tried like a struggler,
like a mismatched warrior pitched into the ring

against a djinn in a den of thieves and cabbalists.
There was nowhere else he could go, save —

CUT TO BLACK:

Tenth arrondissement. The ORCHESTRA has

floated out from the pit.

The brass instruments are furthest, highest,

PLAYERS holding on.

We are drawn towards whatever indifferent force makes its intervention into the

STRUCTURE of things as they are.

Above me, a French horn player clings to his LOVE.

A shower of CENTIMES falls from his pocket, into my face.

CUT TO:

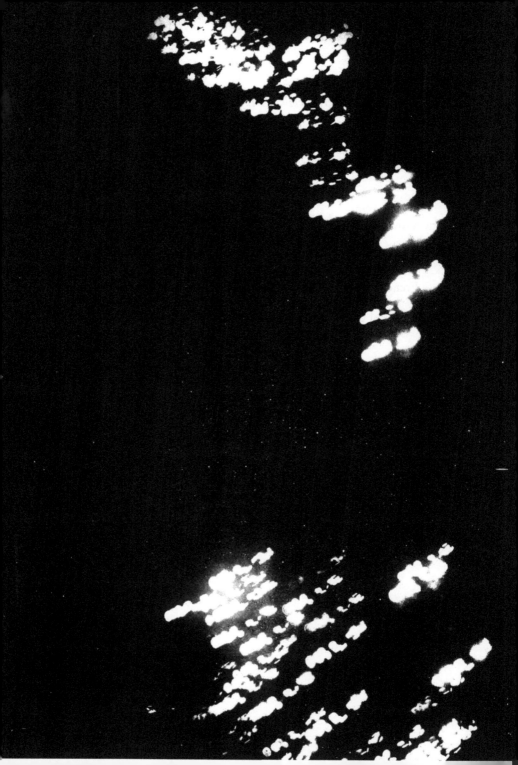

PITCH BLACK.

        Some other time.

                             Airless silence,

as of an unknown

                 COSMOS

        harbouring all

                        we have denied.

        NOW –

distant thunder

        of engines.

        Darkness

                   surges towards light.

        A hundred globes of liquid
        in motion.

Beams flare

        on the vermilion scars
           of this dark artery, underground.

        The sound is UNBEARABLE,

        light bears down.

                    AND –

They are passing.

Inside sleek cockpits,

the DRIVERS,

eyes on the road.

GONE.

We are thrown into SILENCE once more.

The spool begins to CLATTER –

QUICK BLACK

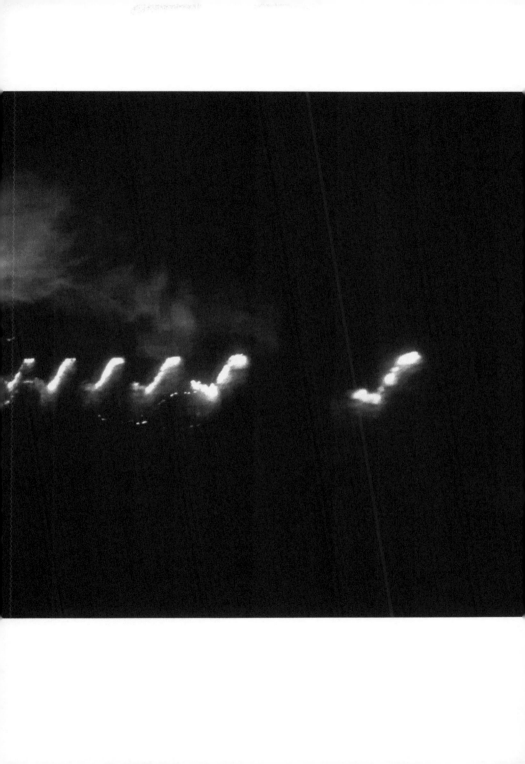

Acknowledgements

I am grateful to:

My family for their love and support.

The Surrealists for flying only a ridiculous flag in the face of all odds; in particular the surrealist artists – Claude Cahun, Ithell Colquhoun and Leonora Carrington – whose own work drew me into new ways of thinking.

Steven J. Fowler and the writers of Popogrou for indispensable wisdom, creative advice and energetic enthusiasm through difficult times.

James Cahill for introducing me to Max and zoological surrealism.

Praise for *Oneiroscope*

'Prepare to be dunked in film. Here's a poetry book, yes it is, that drags you back a century plus, to Paris, or some version of it in Northwest England, and forces you to watch a new thing called cinema. A thing so arresting, so shadowy, that it knows its future might well include making people forget it's so young. What a trick Stephen Sunderland has pulled to make the irrational look static, almost normal. Well, someone did lock him in our house recently, didn't they? Imagine an English in 2023 casting old Surrealist bones and looking real with it? Almost unbelievable, how assured this work is.'

S.J. Fowler
English poet, writer and performer

Author Biography

Stephen Sunderland is the author of surrealist film-novel *The Cinema Beneath the Lake*, three BBC radio dramas – *Ice Dreams*, *Paradise Hazard*, *Phonebreaker* – and two vispo pamphlets, *Eye Movement* (Steel Incisors, 2022) and *Refrains* (forthcoming Steel Incisors, 2023). His work also appears in the anthologies *Seen as Read* (Kingston University Press 2021), *Seeing in Tongues* (forthcoming Steel Incisors, 2023), and in publications such as the feminist-surrealist journal *The Debutante* and *Lune: A Journal of Literary Misrule*.

Find him on Twitter @stephensunderla
and on Mastodon @Corsairsanglot@mastodon.social

About Kingston University Press

Kingston University Press has been publishing high-quality commercial and academic titles since 2009. Our list has always reflected the diverse nature of the student and academic bodies at the university in ways that are designed to impact on debate, to hear new voices, to generate mutual understanding and to complement the values to which the university is committed.

While keeping true to our original mission, and maintaining our wide-ranging backlist titles, our most recent publishing focuses on bringing to the fore voices past and present that reflect and appeal to our community at the university as well as the wider reading community of readers and writers in Kingston, the UK and beyond.

As well as publishing the work of writers and poets from the university's vibrant writing community, we also partner with other disciplines around the university, and organisations from our local community, to bring their content to a wider readership, and publish our own editions of older works.

Our books are all edited, designed and produced by students on Kingston University's MA and BA Publishing courses, whose creativity and publishing skills bring the projects to life.

Follow us on Twitter @KU_press
and Instagram @kingstonuniversitypress

Ingram Content Group UK Ltd.
Milton Keynes UK
UKHW020606050523
421279UK00009B/18

9 781909 362703